From Fractal Fields
Poems of the year twenty-two

by Bob Howse

About the Book

December 21, 2022 :: First Edition

Published in Canada by
Nummist Media :: Halifax, NS
nummist.com

■ ISBN 9780995287839 (paperback)
□ ISBN 9780995287891 (ebook)

Cover art by Janet Howse
Book design by Joseph Howse

Epigraph

How small, of all that human hearts endure,
That part which laws or kings can cause or cure.

—Samuel Johnson (lines contributed to
Oliver Goldsmith's poem, *The Traveller*)

Numbers and Shadows, 2022

Again.
Again, again, again, again
They disappear like grains of sand,
They fall like rain.
. .

Dark and dirty, another baleful rain
Pours from another blackened soul,
Pus-fat in self-regard and craving
Cruelty like a junky's poison needle.
Red it falls and deathly on the rich, black earth,
Drowning it again in blood of innocents
Shed in the anaesthetic sham of greatness
And the blinding gut-rot swill of victimhood,
In this generation, as before,
And before
And before.
. .

Numbers cannot toll the lives, the loss,
Even if the count were truly kept.
Numbers cannot restore the pulses,
The heartbeats, the stolen being
Of 14 million or 1,400 or 14 swept

Into the frenzy of annihilation.
But no one is really counting.
Like the souls they have no power to show,
The numbers, too, are shot and buried
In their shallow graves, below
The barest cover of the thinnest shrug
Of mocking lies in pits with shoddy effort dug.
. .

The special military operation,
Nothing more, nothing less is it
Than a warrant for murder and conquest
Writ in empty words of shit.
But there is nothing special
In a gangster going for genocide
If he rises so high and lives so long,
That nothing true or human will reach him.
. .

Bang, bang, bang, Big Bang.
An infinity of suffering
From a nullity of feeling
In one man, bunkered
By his cult of fear and baubles,
Degrading those who will obey,
Hoping mass murder will not ruin their day,
Hoping they can merely look away.
But when the murder-fury is consumed by its decay,
All ranks of the deluded are together swept away.
. .

The quieter corners of humanity's Hell
Are not so distant from Ukraine.
We live in the shadow of what has been,
We live with the shadow of what can be,
And the shame of what should never be,

And yet may be again.
Again, again, again, again.
. .

Shadow of the shadow of the shadow,
Burning, returning,
Recalled by never learning
That the empty boasts of greatness-lust
Will only grate you down to finest dust,
A speck of lampblack in a dead, dark night
Of countless ashen grains that burned
And gave no light.

What They Knew, 1922

O the waste, what a waste,
What a bleak, blasted waste
Of the land, of the language,
Of the culture, the chaste,
Of a world of old marble
Turned to young rubble,
Classics to garble,
Beliefs shake and wobble,
All patched up in paste.
. .

Old Tom saw this plainly,
He saw it right through
And exposed it arcanely
In the last year twenty-two.
. .

His wasteland was littered
With fragments of Greek;
Generations of students
Didn't know, didn't seek
Any sort of translation
Of these gems of the ages,
Skipped over the squiggles,
Left them locked up in cages,
Didn't know that indifference

Had claimed so many phrases,
Unread and entombed
On pristine, uncut pages.
The same was the fate
Of his snips of Sanskrit.
Hard to feel deep loss
Of what they didn't get.
. .

The pub girls, the demobbed,
The rude and the lewd,
The toothless, the harlot,
The rough and street-shrewd,
All swept like blown litter
Through his dark, fallen city,
Gave voice to the void,
Made his cast for destroyed,
Undone places and faces,
Drained of compass and pity,
Cratered and mired
Like Verdun and the Somme;
Yet who laid this waste?
Weren't they more like Old Tom?
. .

The Lils and the Sweeneys,
They didn't unmake it,
They never were in it;
They didn't forsake it.
It took those who believed it
To end and earthquake it.
Those who knew classics,
Those who read Greek,
Schooled in diplomacy,
Diction, history, to speak
With conviction, persuasion,

Wit and deep thought,
Those who knew better—until they did not.
. .

And now we've come through
To the next twenty-two,
And what a deal of new ruin
Old ruins accrue
If those who know better
Forsake what they knew.
. .

Then what a waste,
What a bleak, blasted waste,
Where the menders?
The healers?
The poets?
The paste?

So Much Depends

It all depends, or so they say.
But not Doc Williams.
. .

For him it was enough to play
A smaller scene, though vivid,
Splashed with rain and colour,
Red, white, slicks and chicks,
Narrowed, barrowed, wheeled
Down to first perceptions.
. .

A field of hues, a glaze,
Things and shapes,
Composed in our perceptions,
Imposed upon our senses,
Implanted in ourselves
And colouring what next
We see and say, feel and do,
Like brushes stirred in water.
. .

So it was with old Matisse,
His goldfish, Persians, aubergines,
There in colour and form to tease
A way of seeing, pleading, please,
Look no more for what it means.

. .

Lily chickens, sunkissed fish,
A barrow red and water
In a bowl or rain or glaze;
So much depends
On how they do amaze
And hold the fleeting eye
As the doctor hurries to his patient
And the painter to his brush
And the people to their rush
To somewhere they surely
Should be going
Before the final hush.
. .

Art is long, life is short,
So many glimpses to import
To make a life of senses
And imprint a sense in life.
. .

So much depends.

She Stops Traffic

She makes them stop and look;
She makes them stop and see
Her colours, forms, and what it took
To bring them forth, set them free
Of her mind's eye, exploding
On a world where they stop time
And traffic, flashing the sublime,
Like a red light or a road man's sign
Coming unexpected upon routine ways,
Seizing the senses, burning off the haze
Of we can't see with the fire of what can be.
. .

But then she always had a knack
For stopping traffic in its track.
Once it was the longhaired girl
Back from London in a miniskirt,
Springing that leggy fashion on the town,
Hitting Spring Garden like a red alert,
Making them stop and look and see
Young life, bright flame and possibility.
. .

And still she can halt the dull rush hour,
The long commute, the enervating power
Of living without looking. With pen

And paint, brush and felt, she feels
A cat, a soul, a glistening lizard that reveals
A bursting world that cries out, "Stop!
Look! This, this is what you're missing;
This is what makes life worth living."
. .

Young are her images born each day,
The fiercely present, the spirits far away,
Love, loss, beauty, endurance, pain, despair,
Have to laugh, have to make, all there,
All possible, all beckoning, all liberating
When she stops traffic.

The Orchardist

Under the eye of Tennant Light,
Above the egg stones and the whaleback shore,
He walks his fractal heathlands
With a pair of pruning shears,
Snips pin cherry, birch, and bay,
Cutting all the dead away,
Helping wild growth grasp new years
And searching out, among the spears
Of crow and juniper-quilted rocks,
Hidden caches of dark, soft earth
Where his seeds and saplings might give birth
To an archipelago of apples, cherries,
Pears and plums and rainbow berries
Broadcast through black spruce and broom,
Where none would ever think to see
A scattered, secret orchard bloom.
. .

But a barren bursts with unlikely life.
On weathered rock it clings and tills.
The bogs and water meadows it fills
With crimson vases enticing prey.
Below a miniature canopy's sway,
Stealthy creatures find their way
On highways hidden from our sight,

To nest and barrow, cave and lair
For pheasant, porcupine, and hare.
. .

Here a glacier left stones for a den,
There a crumbled cellar dug by men
Shelters rabbits in grown-over walls.
Now a pleasant orchard dream calls
Him to walk and prune and plant
His windy heath, so fiercely alive,
Hoping again unlikely life can thrive
And add a few more strokes of wonder
To the canvas lit by Tennant Light.

The Great Rock

The great rock hulks as a sentry in our yard,
Peering over a wetland world of birds and bugs,
A stone-plate shore, a sandy smuggler's cove,
A pepper-mill lighthouse clinging to its perch
Less securely than our Gibraltar knob of granite
Claims its spot, by authority of the glacier
That dropped it there, holding it almost to the last,
As it receded forever, perhaps, into the deep,
And time and earth were no more locked ice-fast.

. .

It is an irresistible sight, this many-tonned erratic,
So oddly named for something so fixed and constant,
Something that is no more likely in future millennia
To up stakes, go walkabout, or spring any surprises,
Than it has in its solid, sedentary vigil of millennia past.
Instead, it draws the world of movement to its mountain,
The gull, osprey, child, tourist, hiker, gardener, neighbour
All compelled to land, to touch, to wonder at its presence.

. .

A child of ice, this rock has since known fire.
A soot-smudged overhang tells years of use
As a burning place, a backyard pyre,
For unwanted stuff and heaped refuse,
Rusted tins, melted glass, a whitewall tire.

At a prehistoric monolith no progress is inferred
By junk of civilization cremated and interred.
. .

An iron dumpster, a lesser glacier, carried off this blight;
Now the great rock is ringed with Joe's fruit trees
And for a while its mass will shield and shelter these
From the sprays and gales that make this place
One no apple, apricot, or pear would volunteer to face.
This time as a towering orchard steward may be long
As seems to me, or to the ripening fruits or spreading trees.
But to the weathered granite carved by ice and wind and seas
It's the work of a small, bright season of bees
And sweet birdsong
Specked in a span of shrouded, glacial, geologic time
That can't be known to those who move about and rhyme.

Shim and Sham

Some say the world
Is yin and yang,
Some make it
Din and bang.
The path I've travelled
To where I am
Suggests to me
It's shim and sham.
. .

The many shams
In which to fall
Want you to think
They say it all,
Will fix you up
With their invention,
Teething problems
Too slight to mention.
Or they alone
Will make life full,
Will be the cure
Of all your woes.
You can be sure
That it's all bull,

Not the way
Life goes.
. .

The way it goes
Is not turnkey;
Life really
Runs on shims,
In-betweens that we
Each time
Must hack or find
To get the rhyme,
To fill the gap
Between what is
And what we want
To make of life
Before we
Make the lap.

NummSquared

I made Sam a little saw,
He made me a computer.
He made the world a language
Of careful logic, axioms, and proof
Because lives hung there
In the code and
Because he cared
Too much to be aloof
To what was hard and needed.
. .

He called it NummSquared.
The provable language
Was his way to aim,
As he knew he must,
At that hardest thing,
To make certain of code
That lives could trust.
. .

Through many tries
And tribulations,
And indifferent doubters
Who would not try,
He made his language
To guide the hands

And make the code
Straight and true,
Not warped or frozen
In loops and discontinuous stew.
. .

Straight and true,
Like a little saw
Pulled with care,
He made NummSquared
Because lives hung there
In the code and
Because he cared.

An Old Felt Hat

He is so far behind the times
He thinks in riddles,
Rhythms, rhymes.
. .
Where are the likes,
The clicks, in that?
You can't go viral
In an old felt hat.
. .
But if a hat
Is by Seurat,
Rhymed by Sondheim,
He shows that
Finishing a hat,
Starting on a hat,
Look, I made a hat
Is the only way to see
Through the window
That must be
Between the hat and me,
Between the world and me,
Traversing this and that.
. .
So many windows

Now are closed,
So many displays,
Output posed,
Seeing shut out,
Away with sense,
Value a tout,
Away with cents,
They crave the coin
Of influence.
. .

A tweet from Elron
And they buy.
And Elron sells
And still they cry
There is no limit
To this sky
And cloud wherein is slyly writ
Value as they imagine it.
. .

A hat of felt,
They do not feel,
Can ever touch
The meta-real,
Where crypto buys
You crypts of zip,
Nothing for nothing,
Fair empty flip.
. .

And yet they chain
Themselves to it,
Prisoned in a void
So vast that
Cannot fill
An old felt hat.

Hard Copy

They do not see
That out of date
Goes back and forth,
Not one way straight.
And who sees that
They rank a fool,
And more than that,
Of an old school
That bound its words
In types and fonts
And points and picas,
Ems and jaunts,
Of serifs, sans,
And Roman ranks.
Ancient, pointless,
Past that, thanks.
. .

Yet hot or cold,
Like rhymes and blanks,
Measured type, finite space
Justified and honed
The thoughts
Which unrestrained
In column lengths

Snaked around
The money spots.
. .

No ad, no comp room
Guideposts now,
No want of space,
No margin cost
Of going on
And going on
And going on
In endless race,
Heedless if the point is lost.
Even if no point is found,
Even if all thought is drowned
In floods and runs unchecked by space,
Never varying the pace,
Going round, round and round,
Keeping on, nothing said
Till the battery is dead.
. .

Easy to think
The past was blind
To vistas of
The tweeting mind,
The fleeting mind,
So full of voice,
So void of song,
So little seeing
Short or long,
Either way,
Back or fore,
Beyond today
An untried door.

Highly Irregular

Bee me no bees,
Flee me no fleas,
Knead me no knees,
Sleaze me no sleaze.
. .

Sigh me no sighs,
Eye me no eyes,
Lie me no lies,
Prise me no prize.

Aelfred Had Me Made

Aelfred mec heht gewyrcan,
So you know who had me made.
Yet you don't know what I am,
Not for sure.

. .

Oh, yes, there are some theories,
That I danced upon a staff
As some ecclesiastic pointed
Out the scrivener's letters
To those who saw just scratches
Next the cartoons on the vellum,
Painted whorls and monsters
That appealed more.

. .

But safe beneath my crystal,
Set in gold and bright enamel
I watch you, still a mystery,
The only one, a riddle,
From a time that loved
Its riddles and its lore.

. .

So whatever was my purpose,
I can say at least I lasted.
Few can say as much

To many, for so long,
Or tell so rich a tale
Without telling what
I'm for.
. .

Now my rock glass is an eye
To draw the generations back
To telling, cunning craft
Of heart and hand;
So let these stand
Reason enough for Aelfred
To have had me made
And give you thought
That aestels and such work
You may dare have made
By your hand or heart,
Or by dint of others',
So endure.

Exeter Eight

Many are my broadcast voices,
Dancing, echoing as in caves.
A song chameleon, I roll the waves
Of shifting, mixing, tumbling,
Cresting melodies in my head.
Now a private, tuneful rumbling,
Now a shriek to wake the dead,
My nature is to mime all nature
And never to hide or mute a note.
. .

An old night-crooner, that's my style,
Bringing bliss to boys downtown.
Soaring, plunging, storming,
Swooning through my songs,
I leave them still as wakeful night,
Drawn to music beyond their sight.
Name me, place me, if you can:
All manner of melodies I jive,
The festive, heroic, and the deep,
An orchestra to make the night alive
And bear you guessing into sleep.

Maximizing

Draca sceal on hlaewe,
Frod, fraetwum wlanc.
. .

You'll find the dragon on his barrow,
Dreadful old and treasure-proud.
You'll find that wisdom in the Maxims,
Old verses that were read aloud
To entertain and let you know
Just how things in this world must go.
. .

So frost must freeze and fire burn wood,
Earth must blossom, hills rise green
When ice is unlocked and the sun is seen
By sprouts that shoot up, starting on
The road to summer, then to harvest,
Days that smuggle life through the cold
When tall trees mourn lost leaves grown old.
. .

So many souls inhabit the earth;
As many are the thoughts and ways
Sprung from their minds, given birth
Like beads from clouds on rainy days.
. .

Raindrops fill lakes, make rivers run;

Rivers must meet and mingle with seas.
Seas bring storms that batter the shore
Till winds cease to rage and rouse them no more,
Like blessed lands freed from the warmonger's roar.
. .

Truth can be tricky and treasure too sticky,
For gold is best given, not hoarded on high.
So share it out, kings; be givers of rings,
Good life is the best crop under the sky.
Good life has a place and a welcome for all;
A hall needs a door and a door needs a hall.
. .

Well-loved is the giver for all that she brings,
And he laments least who fills days with song,
Whose hand can pluck music from resonant strings,
A lift for the senses as life hums us along.

My Father's Squares

I set my father's squares
Up on the bookcase, high,
To watch me unawares,
To watch me as I try.
Wise and well-used, his tools
Tell a life of craft; their jewels
Are blades of steel weathered smooth
By all his years, his works, his toils,
Brass facings, pins, and neat trefoils,
Palm-polished rosewood handles
Too good for my scant skills to use,
So let them perch there as a muse
And be a fine reminder of my Dad
And of how things should be tried
And done: with care and honesty
And finally with precision won.

· ·

In writing, as in building,
You always owe folks that,
Not just the flash and gleam
Of smooth surface and heartstrings.
Tenoned post and mortised beam
Must come first to anchor things.

..

You need a good, strong joint
To hold it all together,
And a true, measured cut
On a line set to a square,
A planted, plumb foundation,
A base that will bear
An argument grounded
In truths discovered there
And in the nature of what is.

..

Dad knew nothing of Pythagoras,
Whose theorem was a stranger too,
But he could make his corners true
By laying out a triangle whose sides
Were multiples of three, four, five.
Hypotenuse was foreign speech to him,
But geometry was, in his rough hands,
An art and language very much alive,
Still there in his antique try squares,
Watching from a bookcase as I strive.

Ralph

Ralph was an artist
In honeyed wood.
He raised his panels
With only a saw,
And fit cupboard arrays
That looked just right
By some internal law
That guided his hand
And satisfied his eye,
Meeting Ralph's test
To which all must defer:
It "took the look off her."
. .

Off to the lumber yard
We would go
To tear apart a pile
Of sugar pine to find
The boards just so
In grain and figure
To make him smile
And suit his knowing mind.
. .

"Wish it were nighttime,"
He'd laugh with a wink

As he framed the case
For our old, blue sink.
He hummed with his saw,
Making treasures each day,
Then tore off for his girl
Down Cape Breton way.

Grampy's Path

My Grampy piled his firewood in perfect walls
That would have pleased a Roman engineer.
He cut the driveway snow in banks
That hugged an absent plumb line, or very near.
. .

He scythed the field in arcs of tumbling hay,
Fashioned a tandem sledge for the day
When he would pull fresh logs from wintry woods.
. .

He loved a step dance, a little song, a silly rhyme,
To make the young ones laugh, and in his time
Jollied us as a juggler, the only one we knew.
He read me the paper the whole way through.
. .

There was a time he kept a store in town,
Close by the river and the iron bridge.
But he had no head for business things
Unless it were the business of curing frown
And plucking twinkles out of stings.
. .

One winter the river jammed
With ice and saved him,
Lifted the bridge, shifted the store,
And fixed it so he sold no more,

But did the harder work of back and hand,
In the lumber mill and on the land,
That let him be merry, helping, and poor.
. .

And later, when his mind would wander,
Or antique sharks would rob him of old treasures,
He made it his business to be a gentle presence,
His little store of fun dispensing pleasures
As best as he could manage to conceive them.
. .

And every end of day, at dusk,
He'd take the little path to Grammy's barn,
Cradling the house cats in his arms,
Ferrying them to beds of straw,
Lodged for night with Grammy's cow,
Content, like him, in gentle now.

Glass Eyes

"Get thee glass eyes," Lear told maimed Gloucester;
"And, like a scurvy politician, seem
To see the things thou dost not."
Not much has changed since then, I thought.
Except there are so many more
On networks, blogs, and foolish apps
To try us with their glass-eyed lies
And multiplying ways and means
To try to make us close our eyes,
Believe their show of what's not there
And be their pipes and fiddles
To play their notes of hate, contempt, and fear.
. .

"Through totter'd rags small vices do appear;
Robes and furr'd gowns hide all."
A hard lesson for a jilted, foolish king.
Today that old authority of silks and furs
Pales beside what a deal on Fox can bring
To a sneering head ready to bluster anything
That juices the ratings with outrage void of truth.
. .

Play to the base with baseness, that's the script.
Play the prophet to the grifted who believe,
Play the entertainer to those you don't deceive

To claim that none should hold you to account
Even as the evils of your poison malice mount.

From Dawn Till Dusk, Elron Busk

From dawn till dusk,
Elron Busk
Tweets his finger
To the bone.
. .
But no one wants
To work
Anymore
Where Elron sleeps
On the floor,
Tweeting them
To be hardcore
As he sweeps them
Out the door.
. .
Now Elron Busk,
From dawn till dusk,
Tweets his finger
To the bone,
Tweeting, tweeting
All alone,
Ranting at

The Apple Store,
Sleeping on
An empty floor,
With only
His iPhone.

Baking Equivalency

In a nation where a baker
Can refuse to make a cake
To celebrate a gay wedding day,
Then surely a phone maker
Can refuse to be the seller
Of an app that is the baker
Of an endless stream of hate,
Though it means the richest man
Can't have his way.

Donors to Owners

Dark money never did one damn good thing
For government of, for, and by the people.
It smothers democratic choice
In sooty, snooty, suffocating clouds.

. .

When secret councils gather to invest
The riches of the self-anointed
In voter outcomes they think best,
Their bankroll is nothing but a noose
Around the voters' necks.

. .

Their manipulations are just another grift
Where slinking, stinking money buys
A grip on power with the biggest lies.
And a people doused in bullshit slips
Into unfreedom where the waiting prize
Is the cruel, returning crack of masters' whips.

. .

Do not be fooled by claims of public good,
Free speech, self-interest guised
As charity, pampered by forgiven tax.
These are the malefactors of great wealth
The old Bull Moose denounced, and if you're lax
These donors would be your owners.

Meta, 2022

For me, there could be nothing worse
Than living in a Metaverse,
A burg from Zuckerberg to nurse
The Facehooked inmates from their last terse,
Faint connection to that open nonline universe
Of living creatures, nature, wonders so diverse
That leaving them for upstart Meta
Would be the greatest sort of curse.

. .

Yet Meta's verse is mired in primordial hype.
Can't say exactly what it is; just sure it's ripe
For commerce in every metanook of metawhere.
And never will the metanaut have to leave his chair.

. .

But, really, meta verses have been better made before.
Two millennia ago, Rome's Ovid perfected these
In the fifteen books of his epic *Metamorphoses*.

. .

I'll tell you, promised Ovid, of old forms made new,
Of beings transformed, illusions revealed,
Disguises unmasked, a universe peeled
Like a savoury orange, bringing love into view.

. .

His poems of love and transformation have endured.

In every generation, reworking his tales has ensured
His stories still thrive somewhere in our living world.
Boccaccio, Chaucer, and Shakespeare all saw fit
To lift good plots from Ovid's verse; and Dante, too, mined it.
In Medieval times, O's classic meta verses were a hit
Long before Z's fuzzy Metaverse could not commit
To more than a buzzword, its solar candle still unlit.
. .

But in a shifty, imperial world, change wasn't Ovid's friend.
Some verse, some theme offended great Augustus
And, on a distant Black Sea shore,
Love's poet met a lonely end.
. .

A world of meta verse or verses may seem to hold escape,
But the living world will pull you back
And therein is your fate.

Tractatus, 1922

Whereof we cannot speak,
Thereof we must be silent.
. .

That was clever Ludwig's view
Of the limits of our logic,
Of our language, and of life,
But all that was the case for him
Is now the case for all too few.
. .

For what would talking heads,
Blog addicts, outrage jockeys do
If Ludwig's limits on saying nil
Cut them into silence like a knife?
. .

When in doubt, leave it out;
Sage advice in green reporters' ears
Chimed by diligent editors
Over endless copy, over countless years.
. .

What do, what can we know?
What can, what should we say?
. .

Scribes must ask that every day
To report what is and only that.

Ludwig asked in the deepest way,
"Standing eye to eye with death,"
Drawing thought like taking breath,
At the front, in prison camp,
Mining Russell, digesting Frege,
Surviving shot and cold and damp,
Making his small, unyielding book
On what has meaning if we look
Carefully and depict just facts
Of which the world is truly made.
And doing that, the account is paid.

A Ride Along the River

There's nothing like a drive along our river
When the last snowmelt fills it to the flood
And the first strong rays of springtime
Dance a ragtime syncopation on its waters,
Tumbling over the granites cast by glaciers,
Sliding to a smooth and sparkling waltz
As the liquid dance floor widens on its way
To Tennant Point, the Light, and Pennant Bay.
. .

Snaking down a spruce-walled, twisty road,
You are surprised by the foaming rapids
And a dark, majestic pond, beckoning hook and rod,
Before the river elbows through a hardwood stand
And races your car along the final stretch
To where the open water punctuates the land.
. .

Past the hobbit cottage, river and ocean
Shake hands and mix, like work and play,
Cape Island lobster craft, back from an early day,
Bobbing with beer boats, outboards, whalers
Out for fun, roaring up the estuary on a run,
Sometimes past the Point and red-cap Light
Where ledges and surf, life and rocks get serious,
Concealing wrecks that failed to match their might.

. .

Up on the sunny road, lines of washing
Catch the wind, signalling life goes on
To sailors and the great grey quarried cliffs
On the far shore, troubled no more
By cutters who chiseled and blasted
Their massive faces into barbered blocks,
Loaded on barges bound for city docks,
White stones to stand on iron ruby rocks.

. .

When the river's freight of fog and snow
Is melted by the first spring golden day,
Senses and spirits are lifted in a way
That always-sunshine dwellers cannot know.

Headlands

Our headland calls you out of doors,
Out of inside, turning inside out
Those mines of mind and cares and chores
That dark you in, pulling the latch
To a wild and wider world where you can catch
A perpetual show of sight and sound and feel.
There, Creation throws its weather dramas about,
Suns and soaks and squeals its colour wheel.
. .

In this outer headland world,
Bound only by the sea's horizons,
The ruffles of rolling coastal heath,
And Hamlet's majestical roof of skies
Fretted in the West with ruby fires,
Earth, air, and ocean vie for the senses
Like hawkers of Tsukiji, Portobello, or once Les Halles,
Their wares the real thing and no pretences,
No fee, no gear, no licence at their stalls.
. .

Summer fills our headland with abundance.
Though its thin, peaty soil is a long investment,
Compounding at near-zero rate of interest,
In time it fills the dips and bowls and crevices
In the undulating granite close below,

Feeding a juniper carpet, a bayberry canopy,
And a riot of blooms and berries in every
Size and hue, extravagant in their growth,
Watered by the ocean's silky fog,
And nurtured by a vast arcade of sunlight
Unhindered by the stunted, scattered spruces
Kept compact by the heathland's steward winds.
. .

So rare and rich and real this open headland
In a time of wired headlands, strung on with devices,
Small and bounded by the conjured plenitude
Of flashy algorithmic simulations, upgraded paper moons,
Designed to keep you in, not draw you out,
To be contented strapped inside your head
Even when the you has been evicted
And your headland is no longer yours,
But just a metered channel through which pours
A stream of thin diversions to which you are addicted.
. .

Admission to these headlands
Surely is too high a price
When your brain is reconfigured
As a seller's output device.

Maintenance

Maintenance
Is always short-changed,
Always plays second
Fiddle to that new build
That somebody wants
For gratification or ego
Or for lack of resistance
To marketing, imagined
Trends, influencers,
Pushy opinion,
And all the bombast
And proper propaganda
Of financial, emotional,
And razzle-dazzle hustle.
. .

Maintenance
Always gets fiddled
In the public budget
To make way for goodies,
Trophies, monuments,
Icons, fads, and fantasies
That someone fantasizes
Are lusted for by voters
Or to make a mark in history

Without much solid
Evidence that what
They feign to know is so.
. .

And all these towering triumphs,
Projects, notions, and bundles of tat
Will later come to crumble,
Weather, wear out, and fall flat
When they face the fiddled, enduring,
Perpetual lack, you guessed it:
Maintenance.
. .

"My name is Ozymandias, king of kings:
Look on my works, ye Mighty, and despair…"
That like me,
You made no
Provision
For their
Perpetual care.

Big and Little

When we are little,
It is a big concern
Of parents and teachers
To see that we learn
What little is
In any given case,
And what is big
In relative terms,
Lest we mistake
Great snakes for worms.

. .

So *Big and Little* is
A fundamental book,
Portal to a knowing look
At an elephant (large)
And a field mouse (small).
And soon anything at all
Is easy in scale to categorize,
Once we are wise on tests of size
And can't be fooled by tricksy lies.

. .

But when we grow big
To adult tall,
Say, five-foot-two

Or six-foot-eight,
There is no book,
No book at all,
To keep us straight
On what is small
And what is great,
Not in our life,
Nor in a world
Where many want
To make us hate,
To make us fear,
Turn off our eyes,
Make them our seer.
. .

And so they label big
Their endless ire and strife,
And try to shrink respect, restraint,
Considered thought, and care
Down to little, down to small,
To magnify their static,
Discontented spectacle of life,
And to squeeze out the vital
Effort to make things work,
And to act with kindness,
Which is what matters most of all.
. .

So grown-up hearts and minds
Could also use a *Big and Little* guide
To help them see life for themselves,
To measure it with care, take it inside,
And work it out with kindness and good will,
And not be distracted by every passing shill
Who thrives on making nonsense of proportion.

In life, it's wise to be alert to tests of size,
To spend your time on what is really big
And waste none of it on puffed-up little lies.

That's a Wrap, Gogo

We are not saints, we are not great,
We did show up, if just to wait.
How many who thunder
Can boast as much?
Attendance can be
An end as such,
One that no-shows
Cannot touch.

About the Author

Bob Howse is a Nova Scotian journalist. A former editor-in-chief of *The Chronicle Herald*, Nova Scotia's daily newspaper, he now works at building with wood, stone, and words in the village of Terence Bay, with wife Jan, a painter, and son Joe, a computer scientist and novelist.

From Fractal Fields is Bob's first book of poems.

To learn more about Bob's work, go online:

- **Nummist Media:** nummist.com

    - **Poetry Books**: nummist.com/poetry